WHO ARE YOU?

by

JERRY SAVELLE

Who Are You?
ISBN 0-9655352-7-4
Copyright © 2000 by Jerry Savelle
P. O. Box 748
Crowley, TX 76036

DEDICATION

In 1998 while touring the continent of Africa, I had the privilege of preaching to the wonderful people of Botswana.

Because they were so receptive to my ministry, I have decided to dedicate this little book to everyone who attended these powerful services.

"Who Are You?" was the title to the first message that I shared with them and their enthusiastic response still blesses me to this day.

May all who read this book catch a glimpse of who they are in Christ Jesus.

Sincerely,

Dr. Jerry Savelle

Who Are You ?

People all over the world have asked the question, "Who am I?" Many people have lost sight of who they are simply because of what others have told them. Many have been told they are a failure, they're a nobody, they're useless and many other hurtful words.

Nobody determines who you are but you! Your circumstances don't determine who you are. Your financial situation doesn't determine who you are. Your appearance doesn't even determine who you are. Today, you're going to find out exactly who you are!

If you don't know who you are, then you will live beneath your privileges as a child of God. If you don't know who you are, you will never enjoy God's best for your life.

I'm not talking about who you were born to in the natural. I'm not talking about your natural father and mother. I'm talking about who you are in Christ Jesus. Keeping you from finding out who you are is one of the major tactics of the enemy to keep you in bondage. God does not care what your color may be! God does not care about your race! God does not care where you were born! He sees you as a potential champion! He actually is able to make champions out of nobodies.

In Exodus chapter 3, we find the story of God appearing unto Moses out of a burning bush.

God called unto him and said, "Moses, Moses." And he said, "Here am I."

God begins to talk to Moses and tells him that He has heard the cry of His people. His people had been afflicted and oppressed. They began to cry for deliverance, and God was about to raise up a deliverer. God cares about afflicted people. God has a heart for people who are oppressed. It's not His will that you live in bondage, that you be afflicted, and oppressed. That is not God's best for your life.

He began to speak to Moses and He said, "I want to use you as a deliverer." Notice what Moses said:

Exodus 3:11 says, **Who am I,** *that I should go unto Pharaoh, and that I should bring forth the children of Israel out of Egypt?*

Moses said, "Who am I?"

Moses asked a question that has been asked down through the ages. "Who am I?"

Well, by the time you finish reading this book, you're going to know exactly who you are.

Who Does God Think You Are?

Who you truly are is not what man thinks. It's not what your relatives think. It's not what society thinks. It's what God thinks that matters. And when you know who you are in Christ, then it changes your outlook on life. It changes your attitude. You begin to think like a winner and not a loser.

I want you to discover your identity in Christ. By stopping us from finding out our true identity, Satan can limit us. When you don't know who you are, Satan controls your mind. When you don't know who you are, Satan controls your finances. When you don't know who you are, Satan controls your destiny!

My people are destroyed for lack of knowledge...

Hosea 4:6

There is an abundance of knowledge in the Bible from Genesis to Revelation. In the Bible you will find out who you are - your true identity. And once you find it out, you will never be the same again! Your days of defeat will be over! Satan will no longer be your master! You will dominate him! You will master him when you know who you are in Christ!

Don't believe what I'm telling you just because I say it. I encourage you to go to the Bible. Find out if what I'm saying is true. Don't take anyone's word for it. Find out what the Bible says for yourself. The Bible is true. God is not a man that He should lie. You owe it to yourself to go to the Bible and study it until it becomes your revelation and not just something you heard Jerry Savelle say!

You Are What God Says You Are!

I once was a man without knowledge. I did not know who I was in Christ, and because of it, I lived a defeated life. I didn't know what God had done for me through the redemptive work of Jesus at Calvary. I didn't know that He had made me the righteousness of God. I didn't know that He had given me authority over the devil. I didn't know I was redeemed from sickness and disease. When you don't know these things, then you live oppressed and you live in slavery to the adversary.

But once you find out who you are in Christ Jesus, then something begins to happen on the inside. There is a power called faith that rises up within you, and it causes you to believe that you are what God says you are! You begin to believe that you can do what God says you can do and you can have what God says you can have!

I found this out over thirty years ago, and I have lived a victorious Christian life ever since. Satan is not my master. He does not control my destiny. I am in charge because I found out who I am.

The Truth Will Set You Free

God has supplied an abundance of knowledge, but through religious tradition, Satan has kept the body of Christ in darkness. Religious tradition blinds the hearts and minds of God's people.

In 2 Corinthians chapter 4, the apostle Paul tells us that *if our Gospel is hidden, then it is hidden from those that are lost and perish.* Satan wants to put blinders over your eyes so that you cannot see. That's what religious tradition does. Jesus said that religious tradition makes the Word of God of no affect in one's life.

It's not religious tradition that will set you free. It's not religious tradition that will heal your body. It's not religious tradition that will set your family free. *It's the truth!* And Jesus said, *"My word is Truth."* The definition of the word "truth" is "the highest form of reality that exists." The Bible is the highest form of reality that exists, and if you know the truth, Jesus said it will make you free!

The more truth you know, the more free you become. The more truth you know, the greater freedom you enjoy. I'm a free man. I live in freedom because *I know the truth and the truth has made me free!*

You too can know the truth. It's not hidden **from** you. It's hidden **for** you! God has put His truth between Genesis and Revelation, and if you are hungry enough for freedom, then you'll get in God's Word. And if you continue in that Word, you will be free.

The Bible tells us in John 8:31-32, *If ye continue in my Word, then are ye my disciples indeed; And ye shall know the truth, and the truth shall make you free.* The only thing that can break the chains of bondage is *truth.* Are you ready to know the truth?

You Are a New Creation

Therefore if any man be in Christ, he is a new creature: old things are passed away; behold, all things are become new.

2 Corinthians 5:17

Once you come to Jesus – once you make Him Lord of your life, then you become a new creation. Your past is forgiven. The literal Greek tells us that you are *a new species of being that never existed before.*

Just like Saul of Tarsus on the road to Damascus - when he met Jesus, his life was changed forever. He became a new creation. Saul died and a new man began to live.

On February 11, 1969, at 3 o'clock in the morning, the old Jerry Savelle died when I met Jesus and a new Jerry Savelle came into existence. I'm not the same man. I don't think like that man. I don't talk like that man.

That man's dead. I'm a new man! The old man lived in defeat. The new man lives in victory! Aren't you glad that Jesus has made you brand new?

You're the Righteousness of God

For he hath made him to be sin for us, who knew no sin; that we might be made the righteousness of God in him.

2 Corinthians 5:21

You are the righteousness of God. Jesus died in your place. He took your sin and He made you righteous with His righteousness.

I know religious tradition says, "There's none righteous - no not one." That was before Jesus went to the cross. When He went to the cross when He died and was raised from the dead, the Bible says, *"We were justified."* You were a sinner, but you were saved by grace and now you are the righteousness of God.

If you're going to live a life of victory, then you must have a revelation of the fact that you are the righteousness of God. You're not righteous because of what you've done. You're righteous because of what Jesus did.

God Hears Your Prayers

The Bible says in Psalm 34:15, *The eyes of the Lord are upon the righteous, and His ears are open unto their cry.* The Bible also says that *the effectual fervent prayer of a righteous man availeth much* (James 5:16). The Amplified Bible says, *it makes tremendous power available [dynamic in its working].* That's what happens to a righteous man when he prays. And you are that righteous man or woman! God's eyes are over you and His ears are open to your prayers. When you pray, heaven stands at attention. When you pray, all the angels are on alert. When you pray, God says, "That's one of Mine. They are the righteousness of God. Let's answer their prayer!"

You can stand in God's presence as though sin has never occurred. You can stand in the presence of God without a sense of fear, guilt or inferiority. You can stand in the presence of God because you are righteous. Jesus made you righteous, and there's not anything that Satan can do about it!

You Are a Joint-heir with Jesus

The Spirit itself beareth witness with our spirit, that we are the children of God: And if children, then heirs; heirs of God, and joint-heirs with Christ; if so be that we suffer with him, that we may be also glorified together.

Romans 8:16-17

That simply means that God is your Father. You're an heir of God. You're a joint-heir with Jesus Christ. That means whatever Jesus gets, you get.

My earthly mother and father had two children. I'm the eldest and I have a sister that is four years younger. When my earthly father passed away and went to heaven, he left us an inheritance. My mother is still alive. I hope she stays alive until Jesus comes! But should she die before the appearing of the Lord, then my sister and I inherit everything that my mother and father would leave. I'm an heir. My sister and I are joint-heirs. Everything they have – we get it – it's ours!

Now let me ask you a question. When do I get my inheritance? When my parents die or when I die? I get my inheritance when **my parents die** – not when I die. Some people think that they only get an inheritance from God when they die. No. You got your inheritance from God when Jesus died! Hallelujah!

You are an heir of God and a joint-heir with Jesus. Jesus is the only person who has ever lived and died and then was raised from the dead to see to it that His Will was carried out so that His joint-heirs get what is coming to them. You're a joint-heir with Jesus. That means you are entitled to healing. It's your inheritance. You're entitled to prosperity. It's your inheritance. You're entitled to victory and success. It's your inheritance. Don't wait until you get to heaven. You can have it now in the name of Jesus!

You Are Abraham's Seed

In Deuteronomy 28 the Bible tells us that if you belong to Christ, then you are Abraham's seed. You are an heir to the promise. You should read Deuteronomy chapter 28 to find out what belongs to you. God promised Abraham that he would be blessed coming in - blessed going out - blessed in the city - blessed in the field - blessed in everything he set his hand to do. He would make him the head and not the tail - above and not beneath! When his enemy comes in one way, God will cause him to flee seven ways. That's just a portion of the blessings of Abraham.

And you are Abraham's seed! (Galatians 3:29). No longer call yourself anything but Abraham's seed. You are the seed of Abraham! Hallelujah! What I'm preaching to you will work in every person in every country. I've watched it work all over the world.

People told me twenty years ago, "It won't work in Kenya!" I've been preaching in Kenya for over twenty years and I've watched people get a revelation of this and go from mud huts to a new house. They go from walking to driving! I've watched it work too many times. It will work in Kenya. It will work in Nigeria. It will work in Ghana! It will work in Zimbabwe! It will work in Botswana. You are the seed of Abraham and it belongs to you . . . wherever you live!

You Are More than a Conqueror

Nay, in all these things we are more than conquerors through him that loved us.

Romans 8:37

No longer look at yourself as a loser. No longer say, "This will not work for me." No longer say, "You don't understand where I come from." Quit saying, "You don't know my background." Quit saying, "You don't know where I was born!" These things make no difference if you're in Christ! If Jesus is Lord, then the Bible declares that YOU ARE MORE THAN A CONQUEROR! HALLELUJAH!

When you have this revelation in your heart, then there can be no more defeat in your life! There can be no more bondage! You will not fail if you know that you are more than a conqueror.

You're a World Overcomer

For whatsoever is born of God overcometh the world: and this is the victory that overcometh the world, even our faith.

1 John 5:4

If you are born again, if you believe Jesus is Lord, if you believe you're born of God, then you are a world overcomer!

Many people today live in defeat because they do not understand the love of God. Some people think that God loves some more than others. Some people think that's the reason some are more blessed than others. Some think that God loves the white man more than the black man. This is not true. God is no respecter of persons. God loves each and every one of us the same. I'm no different from you. You are no different from me. What God's done in my life, He can do for you.

I know what it's like to live in defeat. Back then, I did not know who I was. But I heard the truth **and the truth set me free.** And from that day until this, God has blessed my life. God has placed His favor on my life. It's because I learned who I was. The moment I began to learn this, I began to act upon it and God confirmed His Word with signs following. It didn't happen in a day - it didn't happen overnight. But I continued to stand on God's Word and it happened.

I refused to allow people to talk me out of it. It was mostly "religious people" who tried to tell me that it wouldn't work. People who meant well - people who were sincere - but they were sincerely wrong. They told me that God would make me sick. They told me that God would harm my children. They told me that God loves poverty. But when I went to the Bible, I found out that what they said was a lie, and I chose not to believe them! I chose to believe the Bible. And God's Word came to pass in my life. **I live in divine** health! I'm blessed! I'm free! I'm happy! I'm full of joy! Hallelujah! And you can be too!

You Are Very Special to God

Most people in the world today feel rejected. They've been told things all of their lives that have kept them down and held them back. You may be one of these people that has been held back or oppressed because of what you've been told. You may have been told that you are a nobody. You may have been told that God does not love you. You may have been told that you will never amount to anything. You may have been born in poverty and told that you will always be poor! But if you go to the Bible, you will find out **that's not what God says!** In fact, if you get God in your life, He will elevate things around your life. He will take you from being beneath and cause you to become above. God will take you in His hands and He will clothe you with His Word. Then He will hold you up to the world like a trophy and He will say to the world, "See what My blood can do! See what My name can do! See what My Word can do! See what My spirit can do!"

When I was a young boy, I was very small for my age. When I started school, all the girls were bigger than me! I was called "Little Jerry" because there was always another "Jerry" in our class and the other Jerry was bigger. So the teacher would call me "Little Jerry." I hated being "Little Jerry" because when you're little, people think you're weak. They think you're frail. They think you can't do what the bigger boys can do. And when you're little, there's always someone bigger who likes to bully you so he can prove how big he is. So when you're little, you have to learn to fight. I was always little and the big guys would pick on me.

Sometimes I would come home crying because they would push me around. They were so big, and I was afraid of them. My

Father said to me one day, "Tonight you're going to learn how to protect yourself."

I said "Dad, you don't understand. The boys in my school are much bigger than me! I can't even reach them!"

He said, "Then hit them in their legs so then you can reach them!"

So he taught me how to box. Every night, when he would come home from work, we had a boxing lesson. My Mother didn't like this, but my Father said, "This boy will never run from another fight!"

So I went to school and there was this big bully in my class. He was my age but he was twice my size! He was almost as big as the teacher. He talked big! He pushed people around! He threatened everybody. He took things from others and wouldn't give them back. Then he dared them to fight him! Everybody was afraid of him. When you saw him, you hoped he didn't see you because if he saw you, he would push you and take things from you.

One day, he took something that belonged to me. It was something my Father had given me, and it was very special to me. He would not give it back. He put it in his pocket and walked away. I said, "Give it back!" He said, "Make me, Little Jerry!" He challenged me, and the other boys heard it and gathered around. They were about to see him "kill" Little Jerry. They could hardly wait! So I'm standing there in that circle, and all these boys were watching us. He said, "Make me give it back, Little Jerry," and he pushed me and I fell down. I wanted to cry, but I didn't. Instead, I got back up and said, "Give it to me!" He said, "Make me!" and he pushed me and I fell down again.

I got up one more time and I said, "I'm not running from you today. If you don't give it to me, you and I are going to fight!"

He said, "You're going to fight me? You can't even reach me, Little Jerry!"

So he turned around to say something to the other boys, and while he wasn't looking, I made a fist. When he turned back around, I jumped up and hit him in the nose! Blood was running from his nose. He fell down on his back! No one could believe it! I couldn't even believe it! He was crying! He was bleeding! So I thought, *This is my opportunity.* So I jumped on his chest and punched him again until he begged me to leave him alone!

I said, "Give me what belongs to me!"

He said, "I will if you stop hitting me!"

I said, "Give it to me or I'll hit you again."

He gave it to me and he never took anything from me again. The older we got, the bigger he got. He remained a bully but he never bothered me again. In fact, when he saw me coming, he would walk the other way. Well, Satan is a bully! He talks big. He says he's going to do this and he's going to do that. And he will if you don't know who you are in Christ Jesus. But you are more than a conqueror! When you find out who you are in Christ, Satan will start running the other way.

You're Hand-picked by God

According as he hath chosen us in him before the foundation of the world, that we should be holy and without blame before him in love.

Ephesians 1:4

The Bible says that God has chosen us before the foundation of the world. When you know you've been chosen, it makes you feel special.

Even as [in His love] He chose us [actually picked us out for Himself as His own] in

28

*Christ before the foundation of the world,
that we should be holy (consecrated and set
apart for Him) and blameless in His sight,
even above reproach, before Him in love.*

Ephesians 1:4 (Amplified)

The Apostle Paul used the word "elect".
"We are the elect of God." Do you know what
that means? It means "hand-picked by God."
God hand-picked each and everyone of us!
You're special!

When you fully understand what Paul is
saying, then it causes you to walk in your true
identity. You begin to think, "Why wouldn't
God bless me? Why wouldn't God heal me?
Why wouldn't God give me victory? I'm chosen by God. I'm hand-picked by God. I've
been set apart by God!" That should make you
feel special and have great confidence that
God is going to see you through, no matter
what you're facing today. You're chosen by
God. You're hand-picked. You're set apart!

You're a Special Treasure

But ye are a chosen generation, a royal priesthood, an holy nation, a peculiar people; that ye should show forth the praises of him who hath called you out of darkness into his marvellous light.

1 Peter 2:9

The Bible says we are a peculiar people. Do you know what this word means in the literal Greek? "Peculiar" means "special treasure." What is God saying to us? He's saying that we are chosen, that we are hand-picked, that we are set apart, that we are His special treasure.

Don't ever let anyone tell you again that you are a nobody, that you are no good, or that you're not favored by God. According to the Bible, you are a special treasure!

When you know these things, you can walk with your head up high, with a dance in your step, and with joy in your heart because you know that you know that you know that God is for you. And if God is for you, then no one can successfully be against you!

Fight for What Is Yours

Go to the Bible, study it, read it, pray over it and ask God to reveal to you who you are in Christ Jesus. Once it becomes a revelation, no one can take it away from you. Satan cannot steal from you any longer. Tell him, "You've defeated me for the last time! You've held me back for the last time! I'm the seed of Abraham, I'm an heir of God, I'm entitled to be blessed. I am entitled to health. I'm entitled to prosperity! You're not stealing it from me any longer."

You are a world overcomer. You're not a loser anymore! You're a winner in Christ Jesus! All you have to do is shake your Bible at the devil and tell him, "It is written, I am more than a conqueror in Jesus' Name!"

You're going to find out, when you know who you are, that Satan will flee from you! Satan is a worthy opponent, but he is a defeated foe. Jesus has already beaten him. He has already stripped him of his authority and stripped him of his power! He cannot defeat you any longer. You are more than a conqueror!

Confess right now: "I know who I am. I am a New Creation! I am the righteousness of God! I am a joint-heir with Jesus! I'm an heir of God! I'm more than a conqueror! I'm the seed of Abraham! I'm a world overcomer and from this day forward, I AM A WINNER! HALLELUJAH!"

Dr. Jerry Savelle is a noted author, evangelist, and teacher who travels extensively throughout the United States, Canada, and around the globe. He is president of Jerry Savelle Ministries International, a ministry of many outreaches devoted to meeting the needs of believers all over the world.

Well-known for his balanced Biblical teaching, Dr. Savelle has conducted seminars, crusades and conventions for over thirty years as well as ministered in thousands of churches and fellowships. He is in great demand today because of his inspiring message of victory and faith and his vivid, and often humorous, illustrations from the Bible. He teaches the uncompromised Word of God with a power and an authority that is exciting, but with a love that delivers the message directly to the spirit man.

In addition to his international headquarters in Crowley, Texas, Dr. Savelle is also founder of JSMI-Kenya; JSMI-United

Kingdom; JSMI-South Africa; JSMI-Tanzania; JSMI-Australia; and JSMI-Asia. He is also founder and President of JSMI Bible Institute and School of World Evangelism in the USA, Kenya and the United Kingdom. It is a two-year school for the preparation of ministers to take the Gospel of Jesus Christ to the nations of the world.

In addition, the missions outreach of his ministry extends to over 50 countries around the world.

Dr. Savelle has authored many books and has an extensive video and cassette teaching tape ministry and a worldwide television broadcast. Thousands of books, tapes, and videos are distributed around the world each year through Jerry Savelle Ministries International.

For a complete list of tapes, videos and
books by Jerry Savelle, write or call:

Jerry Savelle Ministries International
P. O. Box 748
Crowley, TX 76036
817/297-3155

Feel free to include your prayer requests
and comments when you write.
Visit us at our website:
www.jsmi.org

Other Books by Jerry Savelle:

Take Charge of Your Financial Destiny

From Devastation To Restoration

Walking In Divine Favor

Turning Your Dreams Into Reality

Turning Your Adversity Into Victory

Honoring Your Heritage Of Faith

Don't Let Go Of Your Dreams

Faith Building Daily Devotionals

The Force Of Joy

*If Satan Can't Steal Your Joy,
He Can't Keep Your Goods*

A Right Mental Attitude

The Nature Of Faith

The Established Heart

Sharing Jesus Effectively

How To Overcome Financial Famine

You're Somebody Special To God

FOR THOSE WHO DON'T KNOW JESUS, WOULD YOU LIKE TO KNOW HIM?

If you were to die today, where would you spend eternity? If you have accepted Jesus Christ as your personal Lord and Savior, you can be assured that when you die, you will go directly into the presence of God in Heaven. If you have not accepted Jesus as your personal Lord and Savior, is there any reason why you can't make Jesus the Lord of your life right now? Please pray this prayer out loud, and as you do, pray with a sincere and trusting heart, and you will be born again.

DEAR GOD IN HEAVEN,

I come to you in the Name of Jesus to receive salvation and eternal life. I believe that Jesus is Your Son. I believe that He died on the cross for my sins, and that You raised Him from the dead. I receive Jesus now into my heart and make Him the Lord of my life. Jesus, come into my heart. I welcome you as my Lord and Savior. Father, I believe Your Word that says I am now saved. I confess with my mouth that I am saved and born again. I am now a child of God.